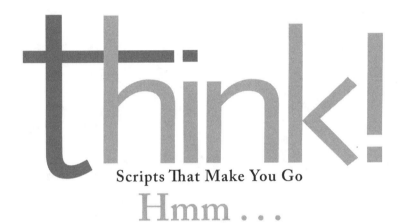

Scripts That Make You Go

Hmm . . .

LILLENAS®

DRAMA

think!

Scripts That Make You Go

Hmm . . .

by onetimeblind

lillenas | PO Box 419527
Kansas City, MO 64141
PUBLISHING COMPANY
a division of nazarene publishing house

Questions? Please write or call:
    Lillenas Publishing Company
    Drama Resources
    P. O. Box 419527
    Kansas City, MO 64141
    Phone: 816-931-1900 • Fax: 816-412-8390
    E-mail: drama@lillenas.com
    Web site: www.lillenasdrama.com

Cover art by Darlene Filley
Interior design by Sharon Page

dedication

"not to us, O Lord, not to us
but to Your name be the glory;
because of Your love and faithfulness."
Psalm 115:1

contents

introduction

Sometimes structure is great; other times it's too restrictive. Structure can guide your mind, but it can also stunt your creativity. When used properly, structure enhances your artistic performance. When carried to an extreme, it surrounds your performance with an air of unreality.

Flexibility, on the other hand, brings a relaxed atmosphere to an otherwise formulated performance. If taken too far, flexibility is disjointed and confusing. When used well, it increases the effectiveness of your message and invites the audience to place themselves within a fluid artistic representation of reality.

The power of visual art is palpable. Throughout history, it has been used to bring clarity and emphasis to the issues and concerns of the day. It is an influential tool that is best served, in our philosophy, by following a basic guide and allowing yourself the creative freedom to bring it alive. The key is in the balance of the two.

The sketches in this book are intended to serve as an outline for your own creativity. The lines given are meant as an example rather than strict instruction. Become familiar with the concept of each sketch more than the specific lines written on the page. The concept is what allows you to become personally involved in the situation. There are key lines that are necessary to every sketch, but there are many lines that are fillers. Think about what you would do in real life if the sketch were really happening. What would you say? What kind of body language would you naturally use? Be conversational. React naturally and casually to the part. Enjoy the freedom to make the sketch your own. You may see a new direction to take the sketch. If so, do it!

In a few of the sketches, you'll notice we incorporated a devil character. Portraying the devil onstage can be intimidating, but it can also be extremely fruitful. Through the character of the devil, you can communicate ideas that make people uncomfortable. People are often drawn to truth by the power of a lie that is exposed or the realization of their own shortcomings. Using a devil character allows you to expose the true nature of the devil. Sometimes he's cunning; other times he's overtly dangerous. He can be funny, witty, sarcastic, or rude. In life, he will be anything he has to be to get people to follow him. Use that knowledge to your advantage. Examine the qualities of the devil and expose him creatively so people will be made more fully aware of their need for God.

Onstage, we represent the devil by using a pair of sunglasses. Sunglasses block out the light and distort reality. The devil shares the same purpose. He aims to block our vision from the light of Christ and distort the true reality of what God intends. The sunglasses serve as a subtle, casual reminder of who the character is and what he's really about. They also bring an air of reality to the words the character is speaking. They're a fashionable accessory, which is much more appealing and inviting to a modern-day audience member than a red suit with horns and a pitchfork.

We hope you enjoy the material on the following pages. Remember, follow the outline of the sketch, which gives you structure, and enjoy the flexibility to make the sketch your own!

commitment

Running Time: 8 minutes

Themes: Commitment, unity, love

Scripture References: Ephesians 4:1-7; 1 Peter 4:8

Synopsis: Two church members have a conversation over what color the church building's carpet should be. The conversation turns into a heated argument, and one person decides to leave the church. He says he is committed to the church but not to the people. The other member then asks him what the difference is.

Cast:
Drew
Ryan

Props: None

(Ryan and Drew walk onstage talking about the new things happening with their church. The conversation leads to talking about the color of the carpet.)

Ryan *(proudly):* I can't believe things are finally moving around here!

Drew: I know. I'm really excited to see a few things change. Change can be good, you know!

Ryan *(agreeing):* Amen to that. The new paint on the walls is really going to brighten things up around here.

Drew: That's true. This huge room is going to open up a whole lot of opportunities. I'll tell you what, though—I'm pretty excited about the carpet!

Ryan: Oh, yeah. The carpet here is so old. It'll look like a new place once we get the new stuff in here. And the blue color is going to really look great! It will pull out the color from the . . .

Drew *(slightly laughing):* Uh, you mean red carpet. *(Looks at Ryan with a smile)* Sorry, I didn't mean to interrupt you. Go ahead.

Ryan *(smiling):* Oh, no, that's OK. But I actually did mean blue carpet. The carpet's going to be blue. *(Acts surprised)* Didn't you know that?

DREW (*surprised and getting a bit upset*): What are you talking about? The carpet's going to be red. Why would we get blue carpet? That doesn't make any sense.

RYAN (*irritated*): Because blue is the color of the sky, which reminds us of heaven. It'll remind us to always look up! (*Looks up toward heaven*)

DREW (*arguing*): But red is the color of Christ's blood that was shed for our sins! We need that constant reminder!

RYAN (*instantly upset and disagreeing*): No way! Red is for the sin of Satan and it should have no part of our sanctuary!

DREW (*agitated*): The carpet (*yelling*) will be *red!*

RYAN (*yelling*): *Blue!*

DREW: *Red!* Blue is the most idiotic thing I've ever heard of!

RYAN: Well, it's going to be blue. We're not having red carpet in this building.

DREW (*fed up with the argument*): Fine! Have it your way. Have your blue carpet. It doesn't matter. I'm leaving!

(DREW *turns and starts to walk away, but is stopped by* RYAN.)

RYAN: Where are you going?

DREW: I just told you—I'm leaving. I'll find another place.

RYAN (*calmer now*): So, that's it?

DREW (*still irritated*): What?

RYAN: We've worked together at this church for over ten years and that's it? You walk out over the color of the carpet?

DREW (*rudely*): It's not just about the carpet. You know that.

RYAN (*confused now*): I don't understand. What's this really about?

DREW: Look, I've been at this church a long time, and it's always the same old junk. Nothing changes. God didn't mean for it to be this hard.

RYAN: Yeah, it's hard sometimes, but we know to expect that. It says so in the Bible.

DREW: Hard yes, but impossible, no. This situation is impossible. We obviously won't agree. It's just not working out, so I'll find another church. It's not a big deal. I'll just find one that's easier to work with—a better fit for me. (*Turns to leave*)

RYAN *(upset):* But I thought you were committed!

DREW *(turning back to face* RYAN*):* I am committed to the church. I'm not committed to you.

*(*DREW *turns and exits SR.)*

RYAN *(watching* DREW *leave, then speaking in a solemn voice):* But what's the difference? *(He stands still a moment more, then exits SL.)*

dating

Running Time: 5 minutes

Theme: Purity

Scripture Reference: Ephesians 5:3

Synopsis: A guy is talking to Jesus about a new girl he's met. He asks Jesus for approval to date her. Jesus responds with a thought-provoking question that takes the guy by surprise. The guy plays it off and proceeds to ask Jesus a series of dating-related questions, each of which potentially compromises his relationship with the Lord. Jesus responds to each question the same way. When the guy persists in disregarding Jesus' answers, Jesus points out he's headed down a dangerous path.

Cast:
　JESUS
　DREW
　LAURA

Props:
　3 chairs

(JESUS *walks onstage and sits in the middle of three chairs set up at CS. Soon after,* DREW *walks on from SR, excited to see* JESUS *because he has something important to talk to Him about.*)

DREW (*excited and nervous*): Oh, Jesus! Have I got something to tell You!

JESUS (*interested*): Really? Well, come sit down and tell Me all about it.

DREW (*sitting in the chair to* JESUS' *right*): I met a girl. (*Pauses, then continues dreamily*) No—an angel.

(JESUS *smiles.*)

DREW: Seriously, I was going to get a drink, and there she was, standing at the water fountain. I almost fell over . . . she is so beautiful. Her name is Laura.

(*While* DREW *is talking,* LAURA *walks on from SL and sits in the chair to the left of* JESUS. DREW *sees her and tells* JESUS *who she is.*)

DREW (*tapping* JESUS *on the leg and whispering*): That's her!

JESUS: That's her, huh?

DREW *(with a big grin):* Yep. What a hottie! *(Looks excitedly at* JESUS*)* Jesus, can I date her?

JESUS *(thoughtfully):* Where will it lead?

DREW *(confused by His response):* OK . . . whatever. How about holding her hand? Can I hold her hand?

JESUS *(again thoughtful):* Where will it lead?

DREW *(smiling):* I don't know. Let's find out.

*(*DREW *glances at* LAURA *then extends his hand toward her in front of* JESUS. LAURA *responds by placing her hand in* DREW*'s.* DREW *reacts enthusiastically to* JESUS*.)*

DREW: This is great! Hey, Jesus, can I put my arm around her?

JESUS *(a little more firmly):* Where will it lead?

DREW *(as if he didn't hear):* Thanks!

*(*DREW *tries to put his arm around* LAURA*, but* JESUS *is in the way.* DREW *pulls* LAURA *up against* JESUS*' shoulder, finally getting annoyed with the limitations of the whole situation.)*

DREW: OK, Jesus. *(Stands and moves his chair a little further SR, then stands behind* JESUS*)* I have an idea. Why don't You and I switch places?

JESUS *(firmly):* No, I don't think that's a good idea.

DREW *(moving* JESUS *off His chair):* Sure it is! Look at it this way—with You over there and Laura and I over here, we won't be in Your way. *(Ushers* JESUS *to the chair off to their right)*

JESUS: What you mean is, I won't be in your way. Drew, please think . . .

DREW *(interrupting):* Jesus, come on. Don't worry. I have everything under control. *(Sits next to* LAURA*, looking at her adoringly)*

JESUS: That's what concerns me.

DREW: Don't worry! I'm still going to talk to You! *(Pauses, looking at* LAURA*, then looking back at* JESUS*)* For example, I was wondering—can I kiss her?

(Before JESUS *can respond,* DREW *moves toward* LAURA *for a kiss.* JESUS *interrupts before they make contact.)*

JESUS *(clearly upset, interrupting):* When will it stop?

DREW (looking at JESUS, annoyed): What?

JESUS (emphatically): When will it stop?

DREW (rudely): Whatever. (Takes LAURA by the arm, speaking to her as he starts to walk away) Come on. Let's go somewhere with a little more privacy.

(DREW and LAURA walk off SL. JESUS sits there for a moment, then walks off SR.)

football

Running Time: 5 minutes

Theme: Being part of the Body

Scripture References: Romans 12:1-2; 1 Corinthians 12:12-27

Synopsis: A football coach tries to pump up his team for the second half of a game and calls for a substitute for an injured player. The substitute player refuses to enter the game because he is scared of getting hurt. The player and coach argue for a while, then the coach gets fed up and calls the water girl to enter the game instead. The coach asks the substitute player why he is on the team if he doesn't want to play in the game.

Cast:
RYAN—Football coach
DREW—Player
LAURA—Water girl
INJURED PLAYER
PARAMEDICS—Two actors

Props:
Clipboard
Bench
Several water bottles
Football helmet

(DREW and LAURA walk onstage. DREW sits down on the bench that is placed at CS. LAURA tries to sit down, but DREW pushes her off.)

DREW *(rudely):* You can't sit here. You're the water girl.

LAURA *(standing up and fiddling with her water jug):* Sorry.

RYAN *(entering):* All right, guys. So we didn't do so well in the first half. We'll take 'em this half. Time for kick-off—let's go!

(The team watches the imaginary field in front of them, cheering. Together, they stop and watch the ball fly through the air. They mimic the runner's movements with their body language, then yell and moan as someone gets hit on the field.)

LAURA *(shielding her eyes):* Oh, that's disgusting.

DREW: Is his head supposed to do that?

RYAN (*taking charge*): OK, let's get the stretcher out there!

DREW (*speaking to nobody in particular*): See, that's why I'm on the bench. That same thing happened to me last year. I'm not about to play again!

RYAN (*speaking to* DREW): All right, we need another player out there. Smith, you're the only one left. We need you to get out there and play.

LAURA (*giving a little cheer*): Come on, Drew! You can do it! You can do it! Put a little muscle to it!

DREW (*sarcastically to* LAURA): Are you a cheerleader now? (*Looking at* RYAN *and stretching out on the bench*) No way, coach. There's no way I'm going out there.

RYAN (*authoritatively*): Yes, you are. Get your helmet, and get going.

DREW: No, coach! Have you seen the size of those guys out there? They're huge! They're twice my size. I'll get clobbered.

(PARAMEDICS *walk across the stage carrying the* INJURED PLAYER. LAURA *cheers, and* RYAN *tells* INJURED PLAYER *he gave a great effort out there.* INJURED PLAYER *waves his hand, and the* PARAMEDICS *carry him offstage.*)

DREW (*to* RYAN): See! I'm not playing! I don't want to get hurt!

RYAN: Drew, I need you to play.

DREW: No way, Coach. Look, my mom just washed my uniform. I don't want to get it dirty. Plus, I look good sitting on the bench. It's comfortable here. I mean, I show up for practices. Isn't that enough?

RYAN (*upset*): I didn't ask for your opinion. Get out there and play the game!

DREW (*defiantly*): I said no. I'm happy where I am.

(*Throughout this conversation,* LAURA *has been listening, every so often encouraging* DREW *to get out there and play. When* DREW *refuses,* RYAN *turns to* LAURA.)

RYAN: Laura!

LAURA: What, Coach?

RYAN: Get a helmet, and get out there.

LAURA (*in disbelief*): Really, Coach?

RYAN (*smiling*): Really. Come on!

DREW (*complaining*): But Coach, she's just the water girl! She can't do any good out there.

(LAURA *hands her water jug to* DREW *as she walks over to* RYAN *and puts on her helmet.*)

RYAN *(encouraging* LAURA*):* Go, go, go! You can do it!

(LAURA *yells excitedly as she takes off running onto the imaginary field. If possible, she runs out through the middle of the audience.*)

DREW *(disbelieving):* Coach, are you nuts? Why did you put her in the game? She's just the water girl!

RYAN: Because I want to use her in the game. I could have used you, but you weren't willing.

DREW *(disregarding his unwillingness):* She's not even a football player!

RYAN: But she's willing to play, and you're not.

DREW *(with an air of self-confidence):* Of course I'm not. I don't want to get hurt. It's rough out there.

RYAN: Drew, why are you on my team if you won't even play in the game?

(RYAN *looks at* DREW *for a moment, then exits. After a brief pause,* DREW *walks off-stage.*)

gay

Running Time: 8 minutes

Themes: Acceptance, judging, forgiveness

Scripture References: Proverbs 15:1-2; Matthew 7:1-2; Luke 10:30-37

Synopsis: A group of friends are talking when two of them start to use language that makes fun of gay people. The third friend starts to feel uncomfortable with the words they're using. They begin to discuss how Christians respond to people who struggle with homosexuality. The uncomfortable friend shows God's desire that we love all people, despite their sin or struggle.

Cast:
 DREW
 TONY
 RYAN

Props: None

(DREW, TONY, *and* RYAN *walk onstage, hanging out and making small talk.*)

DREW: Hey—so how has your week been going, guys?

TONY *(frustrated):* This week's been horrible! It's been one thing after another after another. One night my dad got mad at me just because I was out late. For no reason at all, he just starts yelling at me. I was like, "Dad, stop being such a homo!"

DREW *(surprised):* Wow! You said that to your dad?

TONY: What? No way, I'm not stupid. I said it in my head.

DREW: Oh, right, right. So what else happened?

TONY: Well, I got a speeding ticket; I hit our cat with my car; I was late to work. This week has just been so gay.

RYAN *(sympathetic but puzzled at their choice of words):* Wow. That's a lot of bad stuff.

TONY: Yeah, totally.

DREW: Yeah, well, how do you think I feel? This week my car died, and I had to have my mom drive me around. Do you know how homo it is to have your mom drop you off at work?

RYAN *(feeling uncomfortable but understanding his point)*: That's pretty bad.

TONY *(laughing, then making fun of DREW)*: Ah, dude, you're such a queer! Your mommy drives you around. Ha! Ha!

DREW: Shut up, you homo. At least I didn't run over my sister's cat today.

(They both laugh as RYAN sits silently listening to them, obviously disturbed.)

DREW *(speaking to RYAN)*: What's wrong with you?

RYAN: Well, I was wondering why you guys are always making fun of homosexuals.

TONY *(surprised at RYAN)*: What? What are you talking about? We don't make fun of people.

RYAN: Well, you keep saying things like "gay" and "homo"—that's making fun of people.

DREW: Ryan, that's an expression. It's slang. You know, like "whassup." It's not meant to be taken personally.

RYAN: I know, but you never know who's around who might struggle with something like that.

(DREW and TONY look at each other, then move away from RYAN.)

DREW *(nervously to RYAN)*: Are you gay?

RYAN: No, I'm not gay, but I'm just saying . . .

TONY *(interrupting)*: Oh, that's good. Besides, if you were gay, we would know.

RYAN *(surprised)*: What? How?

DREW *(speaking as if it's obvious)*: Uh, "gay-dar."

TONY *(agreeing)*: That's right. *(TONY puts his hand up on his head like radar that blinks on and off and makes radar noises.)* Homo alert! Homo alert!

DREW *(laughing at TONY)*: Plus, we don't need to worry about that because all of our friends are Christians.

RYAN *(with disbelief)*: Are you saying Christians can't struggle with homosexuality? Christians struggle with all sorts of things.

DREW *(arrogantly):* Not real Christians. Not ones that love the Lord. Being gay is disgusting!

TONY: Yeah, my uncle said we should take all the gays and put them on an island and blow it up! *(Laughs)*

RYAN *(disgusted):* What? Are you kidding me?

DREW *(confidently smirking, agreeing with* TONY*):* Oh yeah, that's a great idea. Praise the Lord! Let's nuke them all.

RYAN: I can't believe you guys. Homosexuality is a real struggle that anyone could have. Besides, I don't think God wants us to judge and condemn people. He told us to love each other—pray and help each other through our struggles!

DREW *(getting tired of* RYAN*'s lecture):* Look, all I'm saying is I've never had a Christian come up to me and tell me they struggle with being a faggot.

RYAN *(looking at* DREW *and waiting for a moment before speaking):* Well, *(pause)* I wonder why.

*(*RYAN *looks at both guys, then leaves the stage. The other two wait a moment, then leave as well.)*

how can you die for me?

Running Time: 5 minutes

Theme: Faith in action

Scripture Reference: James 2:17

Synopsis: A girl tells Jesus she loves Him so much that she would die for Him. As they talk, two of her friends walk up, outraged that there is prayer going on at their school. They persuade her to sign their petition to ban prayer from school. When they leave, Jesus points out that her willingness to die for Him means nothing if she won't even live for Him.

Cast:
> JESUS
> LAURA—Believer
> DREW
> KAT

Props:
> Clipboard
> Paper
> Pen

(JESUS and LAURA *walk onstage together, talking.*)

LAURA *(excitedly):* Jesus, I love You!

JESUS: I love you too!

LAURA *(emphatically):* No, I mean I *really* love You. (*Pauses, thinking, then continues passionately*) I love You so much I would die for You!

JESUS *(smiling):* Really? Laura, that means a lot to Me. Thanks!

(*Just then,* DREW *and* KAT *walk onstage, one of them holding a petition. They are angrily complaining about something unfair that has happened. They see* LAURA *and walk up to her.*)

DREW: Hey, Laura! I'm so glad we found you. Did you see what happened this morning?

KAT *(disgusted):* Yeah, all of those people praying around the flagpole!

LAURA *(excitedly):* Oh yeah, I saw that! It was great! *(Turns to* JESUS *and smiles, then turns back to* DREW *and* KAT.)

DREW *(in disbelief):* Great? It was wrong!

*(*JESUS *tries to pull* LAURA *away, but* LAURA *motions to him to wait.)*

LAURA *(surprised):* It was wrong?

DREW: Yeah! I almost wrecked my car! I was looking out my window *(turns his head as if in his car)* and thought, "What are they doing?" Then I looked ahead of me and, *"Aaahhh!* Big yellow bus!" I couldn't believe it!

LAURA *(confused):* Uh, I don't understand. What's wrong with praying?

KAT: Nothing is wrong with praying, but you can't do it here at school! It's against the law.

LAURA *(glancing at* JESUS, *even more confused):* Against the law?

(Again, JESUS *tries to pull* LAURA *away. She resists, and* JESUS *looks on in disappointment.)*

DREW: Right! That's why we got this petition together. We're trying to ban prayer from school. Right, Kat?

*(*DREW *and* KAT *chant, "Ban Prayer! Ban Prayer! Ban Prayer!" while raising their fists in the air.)*

KAT: This has to be done. It's illegal to have this going on at our school.

LAURA *(puzzled):* But why is it illegal?

KAT: You know how in government class we're learning there is a separation between church and state? Well, when you take a church activity and bring it to a public "state" school, they aren't separate anymore. So, it's our job as Christians to make them separate.

DREW: Yeah, if you let people come in here and start praying, the next thing you know, people will be bringing guns and knives and start killing people and doing whatever they want!

KAT: That's why this petition is so important. All we need are a couple more signatures. *(Hands petition to* LAURA.*)* Here you go. Just sign here.

LAURA *(slightly unsure):* Well . . . you guys are my friends, right?

KAT: Of course we are! *(Points to the petition)* We all signed right here at the top.

DREW: You are a Christian, aren't you?

LAURA *(confidently):* Yeah, of course I am!

DREW: Well, Christians are supposed to obey the laws of the land! We need your help!

LAURA: Well, OK, if you're sure. *(Signs the petition and hands it back to* KAT.*)*

KAT: Great. Thanks, Laura. You won't regret this.

*(*DREW *and* KAT *walk offstage together, excited about their petition being almost complete.)*

LAURA *(calling after them):* Good luck, guys! *(Smiling, she looks at* JESUS, *who is obviously upset. Surprised, she stops smiling.)* What's wrong?

JESUS *(disappointedly):* How can you die for Me when you won't even live for Me?

(After staring at JESUS *for a moment,* LAURA *turns and walks slowly offstage, realizing what she's just done.* JESUS *walks offstage on the opposite side.)*

image is nothing

Running Time: 4 minutes

Themes: Image, materialism, conformity

Scripture References: Exodus 20:3; Mark 10:20-22; Romans 12:2

Synopsis: The devil walks onstage and speaks to the audience about image. Through his dialogue he conveys how impressed he is that people are not concerned about their image. Ultimately, however, he reveals how much importance they actually do place on it.

Cast:
DEVIL—Male wearing dark sunglasses

Props: None

(DEVIL walks onstage and begins to talk to the audience. He sounds friendly, trying to draw the audience in.)

DEVIL *(complimentary):* I like how you guys are set apart. How you stand out and you don't look like other people. You're so strong in your beliefs. That's really impressive.

(He smiles now and then, still trying to make them feel comfortable with him.)

DEVIL: I mean, you read the Bible, and you do what it says. I'm always so impressed by the commitment you Christians have to your God.

(At this point, a bit of sarcasm begins to creep into his voice as he continues to "compliment" them.)

DEVIL: You know—the Bible says, "Do not conform to this world," and you stick to the Word and live by it! *(With a bit more excitement now)* Take your image, for example.

(He gives a brief pause before continuing.)

DEVIL: You don't conform to this world! Image is nothing to you. *(Pauses, then begins his list)* GAP, Abercrombie & Fitch, Hollister . . . *(Pauses again as he lets his words begin to sink in)*

DEVIL: I mean, the world comes at you with some crazy stuff, and you could get caught up in it. But you don't really care about the world and what it has to offer. *(Pauses again before giving another list)* IPod, PSP, the latest ring tones . . .

DEVIL *(more sarcastically):* When it comes to culture, you guys "show the world" that you don't need what's "in" to be cool or feel accepted. You can be an individual. Someone unique, just the way God made you, right?

DEVIL *(after pausing):* Old Navy, Nike, X-box, Hummer . . .

(He gives one final pause, then speaks mockingly.)

DEVIL: You "Christians" are the real "trendsetters," aren't you? Image is nothing? *(One final pause)* Yeah, right.

(He exits the stage.)

you matter

Running Time: 3 minutes

Themes: Uniqueness, using your gifts

Scripture References: Luke 21:4; 1 Corinthians 12:4

Synopsis: Jesus walks onstage and addresses the audience. He encourages them by telling them how much He loves each of them and how He is able to use each of them in unique ways.

Cast:
> JESUS

Props: None

(JESUS walks to the center front of the stage, looking at the audience, and begins his monologue with them. Throughout the monologue, he scans the audience, resting his eyes on different people every now and then.)

JESUS: The enemy knows I'm here. He knows the power I have, and he knows how important you are to Me. I love you. I love you just the way you are.

(After a brief pause, JESUS continues speaking.)

JESUS: Not only do I love you just the way you are—I intentionally made you that way! Do you think you don't have anything to offer? You're wrong.

(JESUS now begins talking about qualities different people have and how He can use each of those for His glory.)

JESUS: Do you have a smile? I can use that.

JESUS *(looking at another part of the audience):* What is it that you have? Is it dancing? I can use that.

JESUS *(again choosing another part of the audience to look at):* Is it energy that you have? I can use that too. *(Lists off a few qualities, glancing around the audience as He mentions each one)* Can you speak? Can you sing? Can you draw?

(He smiles, pauses, then continues.)

JESUS: I can use that. *(Pauses again)* Do you think you don't count? Do you think you're not important? Those ideas aren't from Me. Who are they from? *(Pauses, as if waiting for an answer)* Those ideas are lies from the enemy.

(JESUS continues, speaking firmly and confidently.)

JESUS: I will use you if you will let Me. There are things I can only use you for. Things you were made to do. Ways only you can show others the real Me. I believe it. I believe you can do whatever I ask you to do. You have power. You can make a difference. You matter. I believe it.

(He again pauses, scanning the audience, smiling at the thought that what He's saying is true, yet challenging each of them to believe it also.)

JESUS: But it doesn't matter what I believe. What matters is what you believe.

(He stands there for another moment, then exits the stage.)

kick

Running Time: 7 minutes

Theme: Avoiding temptation

Scripture References: Luke 3:8; James 4:7

Synopsis: Two people are talking when a person comes out of nowhere and kicks one of them in the backside. The kicker denies his actions upon questioning, then kicks again. After a third kick, the angry recipient asks why he keeps kicking him. The kicker explains that he knows he shouldn't do it, but he just keeps putting himself back into the same situation.

Cast:
> DREW
> KAT
> RYAN—Kicker

(DREW *and* KAT *walk onstage.* DREW *is telling* KAT *a story about his aunt. They stop at CS, with* DREW *standing SR and* KAT *standing SL.*)

DREW: Let me tell you what happened last weekend.

KAT *(interested):* What?

DREW: Well, you know my Aunt Ruth—loopy Ruth?

KAT: Yeah. She's the crazy one, right?

DREW: Uh-huh. Well, Aunt Ruth was with some of her friends at a hotel, and she walked into the elevator this one day and . . .

(RYAN *enters from SR, pauses for a moment, then walks up to* DREW *and kicks him. He then walks away, standing to the right of the stage as if nothing happened.*)

KAT *(unaware of the kick):* And what? Drew, what? What's the matter? You were telling me about your aunt.

DREW *(looking at* RYAN*):* That guy just kicked me!

KAT: What? I didn't see anyone kick you. If somebody kicked you, I would have seen it.

DREW: You didn't see that guy kick me? I'm telling you a story and, suddenly, *wham!*—He kicks me!

KAT: You're crazy. Nobody kicked you.

DREW: Either that was a big old fly, or that dude just kicked me! *(Turning to* RYAN*)* Hey, mister, you got a problem?

RYAN *(innocently):* A problem? No! I'm just standing here.

DREW: You just kicked me.

RYAN *(in disbelief):* Kicked you! I didn't kick you.

DREW: Yes, you did. I felt it!

RYAN: I didn't kick you. You're nuts!

KAT *(to* RYAN*):* Yeah, I'm sorry. It runs in his family. He's got a loopy aunt and all.

DREW: Look, mister. Don't kick me again.

RYAN: I don't know what you're talking about.

*(*DREW *resumes his story. Behind him,* RYAN *tries to refrain from kicking him.)*

DREW *(to* KAT*):* Anyway, my aunt's on the elevator, and these three huge guys get on and one says, "Hey lady, hit number four." My aunt dives down to the floor, screaming . . .

*(*RYAN *kicks* DREW. DREW *gets angry.* KAT *steps in.)*

KAT *(excitedly):* Hey, Drew. That guy just kicked you!

DREW *(glaring at* RYAN*):* You don't say!

KAT *(holding* DREW*'s arm):* OK, listen. I don't want to see a fight. Think happy thoughts. Be nice. Just be happy.

DREW *(speaking nicely, trying to control his anger as he walks over to* RYAN*):* Excuse me, kicking boy. *(Using his normal voice)* What's your problem?

RYAN: My problem? What are you talking about? I don't have a problem!

KAT: Look, I just saw you kick him.

RYAN: No, you didn't.

KAT *(insistently):* Yes, I did.

DREW: And I felt it!

RYAN *(giving in):* OK, OK. I admit it. I have a problem with kicking people.

DREW: Duh!

KAT: Yes, you do have a problem.

DREW: Look, mister. You have two strikes. First strike, you lied about kicking me the first time. Second strike, you kicked me again! Now, I'm a nice guy, so I'll give you one more chance. But after three strikes, you're out!

KAT (*moving* RYAN *to the other side of the stage):* OK, how about you stand over here. That way, you won't be tempted to kick anymore. *(Turns to* DREW.*)* I can't believe this guy!

DREW: Yeah, and you didn't believe me!

KAT: Well, I'm sorry. Finish your story.

DREW: OK. So my aunt's on the floor screaming, and this guy says, "Hey lady, what's the matter?"

RYAN (*interrupting):* Uh, it's not very comfortable over there. I think I like it a lot better over here. *(Moves back to original spot onstage)*

DREW (*impatiently):* I'm trying to tell a story!

RYAN: Hey, go ahead. I'm just going to stand over here. And don't worry, no more kicking!

(DREW *turns back to* KAT, *frustrated and annoyed.* RYAN *tries to keep himself from kicking again.)*

DREW: So my aunt says, "Didn't you say 'hit the floor?'" And the guy says, "No, crazy woman. I said, 'hit number four.'" See, he said, "hit number four" instead of "hit the floor," and she got them confused . . .

(RYAN *kicks* DREW; DREW *blows up.)*

DREW (*angrily):* Come on, that's it. You're out of here! I'm gonna clean your clock!

RYAN (*apologetically):* I'm sorry! I didn't mean it. I'm so sorry!

DREW: If you're so sorry, then why do you keep kicking me?

RYAN (*pauses):* I guess I just don't want to stop.

DREW: You don't want to stop?

KAT: Come on, Drew. Let's go somewhere else and talk.

(DREW *and* KAT *walk offstage.* RYAN *turns to address the audience.)*

RYAN: See, I have this problem in my life. There's this sin that I struggle with. I fall into the sin, then ask for forgiveness; but each time, I go right back to the place where it's most tempting. *(Pause)* If you don't want to sin, stop putting yourself back in the same situation.

(RYAN exits.)

live in me

Running Time: 7 minutes

Themes: Authenticity, being real with Jesus

Scripture Reference: Jeremiah 29:11-14

Synopsis: Four friends are hanging out, guessing movie quotes and telling jokes. They are relaxed and having fun with each other until Jesus shows up. When Jesus tries to have fun with them, they become silent and rigidly spiritual, refusing to go any deeper than a surface level with Him. After three of the friends get bored and leave, the fourth friend finally discovers what Jesus has been trying to tell them all along.

Cast:
> Jesus
> Drew
> Laura
> Tony
> Kathlene

Props:
> Joke book

(DREW and LAURA enter from SL, talking. LAURA enters first and stands closest to CS.)

DREW: OK, Laura. I've got one for you. You can get this one.

LAURA: OK, let's hear it.

(TONY walks onstage and joins the conversation, standing to the right of LAURA.)

TONY: Hey! What are you guys doing?

DREW: We're doing movie quotes. OK, Laura, this is an easy quote. You can get this movie.

LAURA: All right. Let's go.

DREW *(in a raspy voice, quoting):* "It came to me, my own, my precious."

LAURA *(thinking):* Um . . .

DREW: Come on. Think.

LAURA: I don't know—*E.T.?*

DREW: *E.T.!*

TONY: What? You've seen all three of these!

LAURA: I don't know. What is it?

DREW: *Lord of the Rings!*

LAURA: *Lord of the Rings?* How am I supposed to know that? What did you do—pick the most obscure quote in the movie?

DREW: Obscure quote? That's the premise of the whole movie. You know, the ring?

TONY: Yeah, the whole movie's about the ring. I can't believe you said *E.T.!*

LAURA: OK, fine. I have a quote for you. Tell me what movie this is from.

TONY: Sure. OK.

LAURA: All right. Here it is. (*Disguising her voice to sound like a tough guy with a Chicago accent*) "Hey, Lucy. That guy botherin' you? I know karate." (*Looks expectantly at* DREW *and* TONY)

(DREW *and* TONY *shake their heads in disbelief.*)

DREW (*looking at* LAURA *like she's crazy*): *While You Were Sleeping.*

LAURA (*excitedly*): Yes! That's right!

TONY: You've gotta be kidding me.

DREW: Laura, you always quote from *While You Were Sleeping.*

LAURA: Well, I like that movie.

TONY: Yes, but every quote you do is from the same movie.

DREW: The object of doing movie quotes is to pick a different movie and try to stump us.

(LAURA *continues to argue with* DREW *while* KATHLENE *enters from SR and talks to* TONY.)

KATHLENE: Hey, Tony! Show me the love. (*Hugs* TONY, *then bumps hips with him while both say, "whoop, whoop." She then walks over to* LAURA, *hugs her, and they both say, "whoop, whoop" while bumping hips.* KATHLENE *then moves toward* DREW.) Hey, Drew! (*Acts as if she's going to hug him*)

DREW (*holding up his hand to stop her*): I don't think so.

KATHLENE *(backing off)*: OK, that's cool. What are you guys doing?

DREW: We're doing movie quotes.

LAURA: Yeah, and I just had a really good one. They both got it right away!

TONY: That's because you always quote from the same movie.

LAURA: I told you, I like that movie. *(Pause)* OK, I have a different quote. See if you can get this one.

DREW: Try to make it a little harder, will you? Remember, you're trying to stump us.

LAURA: Yeah, fine. All right, here it is. *(Again disguises her voice to sound like a tough guy with a Chicago accent.)* "I got Ice Capades. I know a guy." *(Looks at everyone expectantly)*

(TONY and DREW groan and shake their heads.)

DREW: Not again.

TONY *(loudly)*: "You're killin' me, Smalls!"

DREW *(annoyed)*: It's *While You Were Sleeping*.

LAURA: Yes! That's it! You guys are good.

KATHLENE *(taking LAURA by the hands)*: Laura, honey, you always quote from *While You Were Sleeping*. That's the oldest movie in the whole world. Nobody watches it anymore! So, really, you should pick a new movie.

LAURA: But I like that movie!

KATHLENE: I know, but …

TONY *(interrupting)*: OK, OK. I've got a joke.

(DREW, LAURA, and KATHLENE turn toward TONY.)

LAURA: OK, let's hear it.

TONY: Why does a milking stool only have three legs?

DREW: I don't know.

KATHLENE: Why?

TONY: Because the cow has the udder one! *(Laughs)*

(DREW, KATHLENE, and LAURA groan.)

LAURA: Wow, Tony. Your jokes are getting cornier all the time. You know what? I got you a joke book for your birthday, but I'm going to give it to you early because you need some help, buddy. I'll go get it and be right back.

(As LAURA turns to exit SL, DREW, KATHLENE, and TONY move closer together.)

TONY: OK, I've got another one.

(TONY, KATHLENE, and DREW begin stage-talking while LAURA continues offstage. As LAURA leaves, JESUS, who is walking on from SL, meets her. She sees Him, stops dead in her tracks, and takes the form of the cross.)

JESUS: Hey, Laura!

LAURA *(seriously):* "The Lord is my Shepherd, I shall not want. He makes me lie down in green pastures."

JESUS *(with a puzzled look):* Uh, thanks, Laura. That's nice.

(LAURA smiles and nods her head.)

JESUS: So, what are you guys up to? Are you doing movie quotes again? I love that game.

LAURA *(staring straight ahead):* "Amazing grace, how sweet the sound that saved a wretch like me."

JESUS *(confused):* Yeah, that's a great song. *(Pauses, waiting for LAURA to talk to Him, then looks at the others.)* Well, I guess I'm going to go say "Hi" to these guys. I'll catch you later?

LAURA: Hallelujah!

(JESUS walks over to the others on SR while LAURA exits SL. JESUS stands close and listens to TONY's joke as TONY, DREW, and KATHLENE begin talking with full voices once again.)

TONY *(singing):* "I left my heart in Sam Clam's Disco."

(DREW and KATHLENE laugh. JESUS joins in. DREW notices JESUS, runs to the other side of Him, and takes the form of the cross. He calls to KATHLENE and TONY, who then notice JESUS and quickly take the form of the cross.)

TONY *(as he puts his arms up):* Holy!

(Throughout this section, when JESUS turns His back to a person, that person puts down his or her arms, then snaps them back into place when JESUS looks again.)

JESUS (looking puzzled): Did I miss something? What are you guys doing? It's Me. It's Jesus.

(DREW begins humming a worship song.)

JESUS (looking at KATHLENE): Kat? (Looks at DREW) Hey, Drew!

KATHLENE: Lord, we take up our cross every day for You.

TONY: Amen.

JESUS: That's great, but the cross is where it all begins, not ends, right?

TONY: Thou art the beginning and the end, Lord.

KATHLENE: Yes, Lord.

JESUS: Thank you, Tony. Thank you, Kat. Look, I don't get this, guys. I want you to act normal around Me, you know? I want you to be real with Me. (Looks at DREW who is still humming, then walks over to him.) Drew?

(DREW looks at JESUS and starts singing out loud to Him, then smiles and raises his hands in the air.)

JESUS: Thank you, Drew. I like it when you worship Me . . .

DREW (interrupting): Praise the Lord!

JESUS: But right now it just seems like you're putting on a show. It doesn't seem real.

(DREW stops singing, looks at JESUS, and falls to his knees.)

DREW (with hands clasped): Oh, Lord, forgive me for putting on a show.

JESUS: Drew, I forgive you.

DREW (jumping back to his feet and into cross formation again): Praise You for grace!

JESUS (looking back and forth at everyone): All right. Look. Say what you have to say, you know? (Looks at TONY.) Tony, you don't think I want to laugh? Tell Me a joke.

(TONY looks wide-eyed at JESUS.)

JESUS: Just like you did before. Tell Me a joke.

TONY: Um, how great Thou art?

JESUS: That's not a joke, Tony.

TONY: Oh, I'm not worthy.

LAURA (*entering SL, carrying a joke book*): All right, Tony, now this is a good book. Here's a joke for you. Knock, knock . . .

JESUS: Laura! Hey!

LAURA (*looking up and noticing* JESUS): Oh brother. (*Drops the joke book on the floor as she hurriedly takes the form of the cross.*)

JESUS (*staring at* LAURA *in disbelief, then turning to* KATHLENE): Kat, show Me the love!

(KATHLENE *looks confusedly at* JESUS.)

JESUS (*smiling and moving His hips sideways*): Whoop, whoop!

KATHLENE: Um, love is patient. Love is kind. It does not envy. It does not boast. Love thy neighbor as thyself?

JESUS (*frustrated*): All that stuff is true. It's good. Look, I don't want you to just say all these things and act a certain way when I am here. (*Pauses, waiting for a response. When He gets none, He walks to CS.*) Well, if this is all you want, this is all you'll get. (*Takes the form of the cross.*)

(DREW, LAURA, TONY, *and* KATHLENE *silently look at each other, confused by what* JESUS *is doing.*)

TONY (*in a loud whisper*): Pssst! How long do we have to keep our arms up?

LAURA: Forever!

TONY: Forever?

KATHLENE: Yeah, forever!

TONY: I can't do that! No. I can't do that!

LAURA: Yes, you can.

DREW: You can do all things through Christ who strengthens you! Stay there.

KATHLENE: Right.

TONY (*referring to going to the bathroom*): No, I am telling you, I can't do it! I have got to go!

LAURA: You have to hold it.

DREW: Hold it.

TONY (*putting his arms down*): I'm leaving. My eyes are floating!

KATHLENE: That's disgusting!

(TONY *exits SR.*)

DREW (*calling after* TONY): You're in trouble.

KATHLENE: Yeah, that's not good.

(DREW, KATHLENE, *and* LAURA *continue holding their arms up, getting bored as the seconds go by.*)

DREW (*putting his arms behind his head and sighing*): This is boring. Kat?

KATHLENE: Yeah?

DREW: Do you want to go get a slushy?

KATHLENE: Sure! I love slushies.

DREW: Let's go.

KATHLENE: OK.

(DREW *and* KATHLENE *put their arms down and start to exit SR.*)

LAURA: You guys can't leave.

DREW: You just got here. You have to stay.

KATHLENE: No kidding.

(LAURA *continues looking straight ahead. She sighs, puts her arms down, and picks up the joke book, which is lying on the floor. She walks over to* JESUS, *looks at Him and shakes her head, then starts to exit SL. As she leaves,* JESUS *speaks.*)

JESUS (*disguising His voice as a tough guy with a Chicago accent*): "I got Ice Capades!"

(LAURA *stops and turns toward Him in surprise.*)

JESUS (*shrugging, again disguising His voice*): "I know a guy."

LAURA (*laughing*): I'm sorry?

JESUS (*smiling*): Hey, do you remember that part in *While You Were Sleeping* where Jack asks Lucy to marry him, and his grandma makes him go inside the toll booth? Then she says, "Get down on one knee!" That was hilarious. That is my favorite part of the movie.

LAURA (*surprised*): Your favorite part? You mean You've seen the movie?

JESUS: Of course I've seen it. It is your favorite movie, right?

LAURA: Yeah.

JESUS: And it's important to you?

LAURA: Well, yeah, I guess.

JESUS: You know, they should come out with a collectors' edition DVD. Something that has bloopers and behind the scenes footage.

LAURA: Oh yeah! And interviews with the cast!

JESUS: That was a great cast.

LAURA: They should do a sequel.

JESUS: Sure. *(Pauses, thinking)* They could call it *While You Slept*.

LAURA *(excitedly):* That's a great idea! Hey, remember that part where Lucy is eating Oreo cookies in her apartment, and she dunks them in her cat's milk? That was so cool.

JESUS: That was disgusting.

LAURA: And then the part where she was decorating her Christmas tree. I love that part because I love Christmas . . .

JESUS *(looking lovingly at* LAURA*):* I know you do.

LAURA *(continuing her thought):* With all the lights and cocoa and presents and snow . . . *(Notices* JESUS *staring at her)* Why are You looking at me like that?

JESUS: Isn't this great? You and Me—talking?

LAURA: Yeah, it's nice.

JESUS: This is the way it's supposed to be.

LAURA: The way what's supposed to be?

JESUS: You. Me. Us. Now we can really dig in deep.

LAURA: Dig in deep to what?

JESUS: Into who you are!

LAURA: OK, Jesus, I already know who I am, so no need to dig.

JESUS: No, I'm sorry, Laura, but you don't have a clue. I know everything about you, Laura. I know things about you that you haven't even discovered yet. But you have this idea that you have to be someone different when we're together. Like you have to say something special or act a certain way, or put on some kind of a show. I just want you to be real with Me all the time.

LAURA: Well, Jesus, I am. I mean, I am always living for You.

JESUS: Yes, but Laura, I don't want you to live for Me. I want you to live *in* Me. It's when you live in Me that you will understand who you really are, and what you're truly living for. *(Looks at* LAURA *for a moment.)* Come on. *(Takes her by the arm and leads her off SR.)*

more coke

Running Time: 7 minutes

Theme: Comparison

Scripture Reference: James 1:17

Synopsis: Jesus surprises two people with gifts He picked out especially for them. The first person loves her gift until she sees what Jesus gave her friend. She rudely demands for Jesus to give her the same thing. She continues to demand more as she sees others walk by with seemingly bigger gifts. Jesus continually insists the value lies not in the gift itself but in His desire for her to have it. She refuses to listen. Jesus finally takes her gift back, telling her she won't understand what the gift really means until she looks past the gift itself.

Cast:
>   Jesus
>   Drew
>   Laura
>   Kat

Props:
>   2 identical gift bags
>   Four-ounce or eight-ounce can of Coke
>   2 twenty-ounce bottles of Coke
>   2 one-liter bottles of Coke
>   Three-liter bottle of Coke (may need to make one using a dark generic soda and the labels from two, two-liter bottles of Coke)
>   2 chairs

(Jesus *walks onstage and places two identically wrapped gift bags on two chairs placed at CS. He places* Drew's *gift (a twenty-ounce bottle of Coke) on the right chair and* Laura's *gift (an eight-ounce can of Coke) on the left chair. He calls to* Laura *and* Drew *to come out, then walks over to SR to guide them, telling them not to peek. They walk to CS, with* Jesus *holding* Laura's *hand and* Laura *holding* Drew's *hand.* Jesus *stops* Drew *on the right side of the chairs. He positions* Laura *on the left side. He stands centered behind the two chairs.)*

Jesus *(excitedly):* OK. Open your eyes!

(LAURA *and* DREW *open their eyes and look around, trying to figure out what* JESUS *wants them to see. They notice the two gift bags and question* JESUS.)

LAURA: What is this?

DREW: Yeah, are these for us?

JESUS *(pleased):* They're gifts—for you, from Me.

DREW: What's the special occasion?

JESUS: No occasion. I just wanted to give you these gifts. I picked them out especially for each of you.

LAURA: You got us gifts for no reason? That is so sweet! You're the best!

DREW: Yeah, and look, they're even wrapped!

JESUS: Do you like the gift bags? I picked them out myself.

(LAURA *and* DREW *continue to comment on how nice it is for* JESUS *to give them gifts.*)

JESUS: Well, Laura, let's have you open your gift.

LAURA: OK. *(Starts to peek inside)* Man, Jesus, I have no idea what You could have gotten me. *(Grabs the eight-ounce can of Coke and pulls it out excitedly)* An eight-ounce can of Coke! Jesus, I love it! This is the best!

JESUS *(pleased):* Do you like it?

LAURA: I love it! This is perfect for me. Look, it's so tiny and cute and perfect!

JESUS *(smiling):* I'm glad you like it. I picked it out myself, just for you.

LAURA: Well, You did a good job, Jesus. You know me so well!

(JESUS *gives* LAURA *a hug.* LAURA *continues to admire her gift as* JESUS *turns to* DREW.)

JESUS *(smiling):* OK, Drew. Open your gift.

DREW: All right. *(Reaches into his bag, wondering what* JESUS *could have gotten for him. He grabs the twenty-ounce bottle of Coke and pulls it out, incredibly excited.)* A twenty-ounce bottle of Coke! Jesus, this is awesome! Look how big this thing is!

JESUS: So you like it?

DREW: I love it! *(Hugs* JESUS*)*

(LAURA *is staring at* DREW's *gift as if she is shocked and upset, looking at her own can then looking at* DREW's *bottle in disgust.*)

DREW: This is great for me! I mean, Laura, you got eight ounces, but look at this—twenty whole ounces of Coke!

LAURA *(with little excitement):* Yeah, I see that. That's great.

(JESUS is pleased the two like their gifts. He continues to watch them, excited for them to realize how special they are to him.)

DREW: Thanks, Jesus! Hey, Laura. Let's go show Darryl what we got. *(Turns and walks off SR.)*

LAURA *(somewhat sarcastically):* Yeah, let's go show him. Thanks a lot, Jesus. *(Starts to follow DREW offstage, looking at her can of Coke as if it's nothing.)*

JESUS *(concerned):* Laura.

LAURA *(stops, turns around):* What?

JESUS: Is something wrong?

LAURA *(defensively):* No. Nothing's wrong. Why? Should something be wrong?

JESUS: You just don't seem very happy. What's wrong?

LAURA *(rudely):* There's nothing wrong!

JESUS: Laura, I know something's bothering you. What is it?

LAURA: Fine. If You really want to know, I just don't understand what happened. I mean, I opened my gift and, wow, a cute little eight-ounce can of Coke. Then Drew opened his gift and, hello, twenty ounces! What's the deal?

JESUS: What do you mean? Your gift was for you, and his gift was for him.

LAURA *(glaring at JESUS):* Look, Jesus. This happens all the time. Whenever You give us gifts, Drew always gets more. It's not fair.

JESUS: It's not about who gets more. The important thing is that I picked this gift out especially for you. I wanted you to have it.

LAURA *(exasperated):* It's just not fair! For once, I want You to give me what You gave Drew.

JESUS *(puzzled):* You want Drew's gift?

LAURA: Yes!

JESUS: But that was for him. I picked your gift out for you. That's what I want you to have.

LAURA (with attitude): Just give me what You gave Drew!

(JESUS looks sadly at LAURA, then walks off SL to get a twenty-ounce bottle of Coke. As He leaves, LAURA sits down, staring at her can of Coke, wondering how in the world JESUS could think she'd be satisfied with it. As LAURA sits, KAT walks on from SL, drinking from a one-liter bottle of Coke. LAURA sees it and stops her.)

LAURA: Hey, Kat, what is that?

KAT (holds up bottle): This? (Dreamily) This is one whole liter of God's nectar.

LAURA: Yeah, I can see that. One liter! How are you going to drink all that? That's a lot of Coke!

KAT: Oh no. I love Coke! (Takes another drink, savoring it)

LAURA: Where in the world did you get that, anyway?

KAT (cheerfully): Oh! Jesus got this for me!

LAURA (deflated): Really!

KAT: Yeah, isn't it great? He's awesome! (Starts to walk off SR, still enjoying her Coke)

LAURA: Hey, Kat!

KAT (turning around): Yes?

LAURA: I bet you wouldn't like that Coke so much if you ran into somebody who had a bigger bottle!

KAT: Sure I would. Jesus gave this to me! That would be selfish. (Turns around and walks offstage)

(LAURA stares disbelievingly at KAT, then looks back at her Coke, clearly not satisfied. JESUS walks back onstage, holding a twenty-ounce bottle of Coke out to LAURA, looking at her with anticipation, hoping she'll like it.)

JESUS (cheerfully): Here you go!

LAURA (moodily): What is that?

JESUS (smiling): It's a twenty-ounce bottle of Coke, just like you wanted.

LAURA: Well, Kat just came by.

JESUS: Oh yeah?

LAURA: Yeah! Drinking the one-liter Coke she said You got her!

JESUS: Yeah, that's the gift I gave to Kat.

LAURA *(shaking her head):* Look, are You mad at me or something? Did I do something wrong? Did I make you mad?

JESUS: No. Why?

LAURA: Why does Kat get a one-liter bottle of Coke? This is ridiculous! I told You, You always give other people more than You give me.

JESUS *(holding out the twenty-ounce bottle):* You said you wanted the gift I gave Drew. This is what I gave him. Here it is.

LAURA *(rudely):* Well, that was before I saw what Kat has. I want what Kat has!

JESUS: You want what Kat has?

LAURA *(exasperated):* Yes! Give me what Kat has!

(JESUS shakes His head, saddened by LAURA's refusal to accept what He wants for her. He walks off SL to get a one-liter bottle of Coke for LAURA. As He leaves, LAURA again looks disappointedly at her can of Coke. DREW enters again from SR, now drinking a three-liter Coke. LAURA sees it and is instantly outraged.)

LAURA: Drew! Where in the world did you get that?

DREW: I know! Isn't it great? It's three whole liters!

LAURA *(angrily):* Why do you have a three-liter Coke?

DREW: Oh, Jesus gave me an upgrade!

LAURA *(rolling her eyes):* An upgrade? Come on. That's ridiculous.

DREW: Yeah, I didn't know they came this big either. He must have done some kind of miracle or something.

LAURA: Yeah, well, there's no way you're going to drink all that.

DREW *(laughing):* I know! Hey! *(Notices the can LAURA is still holding)* Oh, nice. You still have that little two-ounce can of Coke. Good for you. *(Grabs it out of LAURA's hand)*

LAURA *(grabbing the can back):* Actually, it's eight ounces.

DREW: Oh, yeah, whatever. That really is perfect for you. It's all tiny and petite, just like you! Hey, it's so tiny—it's like communion-cup size. I bet you could fit twenty of those in my three-liter!

(DREW walks off SL, enjoying his little joke, as LAURA glares after him, insulted. As LAURA again looks at her gift angrily, DREW passes JESUS walking back onstage and

thanks Him for the gift. JESUS *continues over to* LAURA, *carrying a one-liter bottle of Coke to give her. He holds the bottle behind His back as He approaches.)*

JESUS: OK, close your eyes!

LAURA *(disagreeably):* Close my eyes? For what?

JESUS: Here's the one-liter bottle of Coke you wanted! *(Holds it out to her)*

LAURA *(glaring at* JESUS*):* Look, Jesus, are You holding back Your best from me on purpose?

JESUS: What do you mean? You wanted this gift; now here it is.

LAURA: Who cares! Drew just came by—again.

JESUS *(shaking His head as if He cannot believe this):* Oh no.

LAURA: Yeah! With a three-liter Coke he says You got him! What is the deal?

JESUS: That gift was for him. I picked it out for him.

LAURA: Obviously it was for him! First, You give him more than me; now, You give him even more! It's completely unfair. I want what Drew has. Or better yet, I want something bigger. Like a five-liter or a ten-liter. Just give me something bigger than what anyone else has!

JESUS *(frustrated):* Don't you see what is happening here? You're comparing your gift to everyone else's, and it's stealing your joy.

LAURA: No, no, no. What's stealing my joy is that You give everyone else more than You give me!

JESUS: I gave you a gift I picked out for you. You wanted Drew's gift. I gave you what I gave Drew. You wanted Kat's gift. I have what I gave Kat right here; now you want something bigger!

LAURA *(with much attitude):* Of course I do! Just give me something bigger!

JESUS *(pointing at the gift He gave* LAURA*)*: Laura, I picked this out for you. That's what I want you to see.

LAURA *(defiantly):* I don't care!

JESUS *(taking the eight-ounce can from* LAURA *and holding it up at face level between them):* Until you can look past this, all you're going to see is a can of Coke.

*(*LAURA *stares at* JESUS, *then stomps her foot and angrily walks off SR.* JESUS *watches her leave then walks off SL.)*

trash

Running Time: Three 4-minute sections (12 minutes total)

Theme: Releasing your baggage to Jesus

Scripture Reference: Matthew 11:28-30

Synopsis: In this three-part series of scripts, Jesus demonstrates His desire to take the burden of sin from the lives of His people. Two people meet Him and are faced with the decision to lay the trash they've collected at His feet. In *Part One*, the guy and girl see Jesus. The guy immediately recognizes Jesus and throws his trash down. The girl refuses to have anything to do with Jesus. In *Part Two*, the guy convinces the girl to experience the freedom of getting rid of her trash. She lays it down, only to rummage through the smelly bags to retrieve her guilt. In *Part Three*, the girl comes face-to-face with how much Jesus loves her, at last finding freedom from a life burdened by sin and guilt, by accepting Jesus' grace. This series fits nicely into a longer drama presentation but may be adapted to fit in a church service setting. It is helpful to separate each section with other skits or songs.

Cast:
>   JESUS
>   KAT
>   DREW

Props:
>   3 trash bags filled with items that make them bulky (blankets work nicely)
>   Jar of guilt (unbreakable jar filled with dirt or something that looks disgusting)

Part One

(JESUS *walks onstage and stands in the center, waiting.* DREW *and* KAT *walk onstage carrying a heavy trash bag over each of their shoulders.* DREW *walks on first, talking to* KAT *as they walk.*)

DREW *(uncomfortable from his heavy load):* Ugh. I don't know why I hang around you. Man, you smell nasty!

KAT *(also tired and uncomfortable):* Me! You're the one who stinks!

DREW: That's not me you're smelling. *(Sees* JESUS *and stops)*

JESUS *(smiling):* Hey, Drew. It's time.

DREW *(in awe):* Jesus?

KAT *(confused):* Who?

JESUS: It's time. Give me your trash.

DREW *(as if he can't believe it):* Really? *(Starts to walk toward* JESUS*)*

KAT *(puzzled):* Drew, what are you doing? We need to go this way. *(Points in the opposite direction)*

DREW *(addressing* KAT*):* Just a second. *(Turns to* JESUS*)* Are you serious? Just give You my trash?

JESUS *(encouraging* DREW*):* Throw it down right here. I'll take it.

DREW: Sweet! *(Walks over, throws down an obviously heavy burden, and becomes excited)*

KAT *(confused):* What are you doing? You dropped your trash!

DREW *(gradually getting more excited as he realizes he's free):* I didn't drop it; I threw it! It's incredible! *(Lets out a yell of freedom)* Kat, you've got to try it.

KAT *(pretending she doesn't know he's referring to the trash):* Try what? Are you crazy? Pick up your trash, and let's go.

DREW: No way! Kat, come here and get rid of it. Throw down your trash!

KAT: You're out of your mind.

JESUS *(encouraging her):* Come on, Kat. You can do it.

KAT: Why do You want my trash?

JESUS: That's My job. I take people's trash. Please, Kat, give Me your trash.

DREW: Come on, Kat. Chuck it!

KAT: Look, I don't know what Your angle is, but I'm not falling for it. Thanks, but no thanks. *(She walks offstage.)*

*(*DREW *follows* KAT *offstage as he continues encouraging her to give up her trash.)*

JESUS *(watching them leave):* I'll be waiting for you.

(He walks offstage carrying DREW*'s bag of trash.)*

Part Two

(JESUS walks onstage, again waiting for KAT and DREW as they walk onstage. This time, KAT has two garbage bags slung over her shoulder. One bag has the jar of guilt inside. DREW follows behind KAT, still talking about her smelly trash.)

DREW: This is getting out of control. Look at you. The flies won't even hang around you anymore.

KAT: Very funny. If I'm that nasty, why are you still around?

DREW: I'm not giving up on you.

(They see JESUS. DREW is relieved. KAT is annoyed.)

DREW: Look! Here's your chance.

KAT *(sarcastically):* Oh great.

JESUS *(addressing KAT):* I knew you'd be back.

KAT: I'm not back.

DREW: Sure she is.

JESUS: It's time, Kat. Give Me your trash.

KAT *(stopping):* See, this is what I don't get. Why would You want this nasty trash of mine? I made it, so I should live with it.

JESUS: That's the beauty of it. I'll take the trash so you won't have to live with it.

KAT *(confused):* It doesn't make any sense.

DREW: It's like I said before. You're not going to understand it until you experience it for yourself. Let the trash go, then you'll understand.

KAT *(thinking but apprehensive):* I don't know.

DREW: I'll tell you what. I'll make a deal with you. If you give up your trash, and there is no change whatsoever, you can pick the trash back up and I'll stop bothering you.

KAT *(intrigued):* Promise?

DREW: Yep.

JESUS *(smiling):* Go ahead, Kat. Just give me your trash.

KAT: All right, but if there is no change, it's over, understand?

51

(KAT *walks toward* JESUS, *stumbling as she slings her trash over her shoulder and lays it at His feet.*)

JESUS: Are you OK?

KAT (*slowly standing, rubbing her arms*): Yeah, I'm fine.

DREW (*noticing* KAT's *movements*): Doesn't that feel great? OK, shake if off.

(*After a brief moment of feeling awkward,* KAT *allows* DREW *to help her celebrate her freedom.* JESUS *picks up the trash and starts to take it offstage.* KAT *gets scared about feeling so good. She walks toward* JESUS, *grabs the trash and pulls it down to the ground.*)

KAT (*desperately*): Wait a minute. I need something out of there.

DREW (*confused*): What are you doing? You were doing so well.

KAT (*distracted*): I know. (*Opens the bags, searching*) I just need to get something.

(JESUS *and* DREW *react to the terrible smell coming from the trash as* KAT *searches through the bags, finally pulling out the jar of guilt.*)

JESUS: Please, Kat, leave that in there. I want that too.

KAT (*holding the jar close to her*): You can have everything else, but not this. This is mine.

DREW: I'm confused. What is that?

KAT (*possessively*): This is my guilt.

DREW: I'm so proud of you for giving up your trash. I think you should put that with it. You don't need it anymore.

KAT (*angrily*): I am so sick and tired of you telling me what to do all the time. I'm not perfect like you!

DREW (*upset*): I'm not perfect. I'm just trying to help. I want . . .

KAT (*interrupting*): Stop! I've had enough. Don't talk to me anymore. Just leave me alone. (*She walks offstage, angry.*)

(DREW *walks offstage, perplexed, as* JESUS *picks up the trash bags and also walks offstage.*)

Part Three

(JESUS *walks onstage, once more waiting for* KAT, *who walks onstage carrying her jar of guilt. She is sad and depressed.* JESUS *calls to her.*)

JESUS (gently): Kat.

KAT (annoyed): I don't believe this. (Turns to leave)

JESUS: Wait. Please, Kat. Wait and listen to Me.

KAT (stopping): What do You want?

JESUS (softly, lovingly): I know you're scared. I know you're still burdened. Give Me that burden, and I'll pour My grace on you. I'll fill you with peace. I'll show you a love you have never experienced before. Let Me show you how great life can be through Me. I can do more for you than you could possibly imagine. Please. Give Me your guilt.

KAT (resistant): I don't deserve all of those good things. (Holds up her guilt) This is what I deserve.

JESUS (gently but firmly): I'm not counting your sins against you. I'm here to free you from them. I love you. I want to take away the pain you're suffering. I gave up everything so I could gain your love. Don't deny me, Kat. Give Me your guilt. Come to Me.

(As JESUS speaks, KAT realizes His words are true. She pauses, thinking, and recognizes how stubborn she's been. She slowly goes to JESUS at last, humble and broken.)

KAT (with emotion): I'm sorry. (Falls to her knees with her face to the ground, placing her guilt before JESUS.) I'm so sorry, Jesus. I want You to have everything—all of my trash—all of my guilt. I'm so sorry.

(JESUS takes KAT's guilt and sets it aside. He bends down and lifts her up.)

JESUS (looking her in the eyes): I forgive you. (Hugs her) I love you. Walk with Me.

(JESUS and KAT walk offstage together.)

wash my feet

Running Time: 5 minutes

Themes: Service, humility

Scripture Reference: Matthew 20:26-28

Synopsis: Three people announce to the audience the reasons each of them should be considered the greatest person in the world. As they boast about themselves, they argue with each other, pushing each other out of the way and talking loudly. Jesus walks onstage with a bowl of water and a towel, sits each of them on a chair, and proceeds to wash their feet. After demonstrating His act of service, He encourages them to do the same.

Cast:
>   JESUS
>   KAT
>   LAURA
>   DREW

Props:
>   Bowl of water
>   Towel
>   3 chairs

(KAT walks onstage, stands at CS, and addresses the audience.)

KAT *(confidently):* I am the greatest because I trust Jesus the most. I trust Him more than anyone else. So, since I trust Him so much, I'm going to help you learn how to trust Him.

(As KAT continues talking, DREW walks onstage, pushes her aside, and begins his own speech about how great he is.)

DREW *(interrupting):* I am the greatest because I am the greatest Christian leader to ever walk the face of this earth!

KAT *(pushing DREW out of the way):* No, I am the greatest. People, come on up here and form two lines, and I'll teach you how to trust.

DREW *(pushing KAT away):* I lead more people to Jesus than Jesus does!

(As they argue, LAURA walks onstage, pushes both of them out of the way, and tells the audience why she is the greatest.)

LAURA: I am the greatest because I am obviously the most humble servant in the entire world!

(KAT *pushes* LAURA *out of the way, fighting for center stage.* DREW *continues telling the audience about his greatness.*)

KAT *(to* LAURA*):* You are not the greatest. I'm the greatest. I trust Jesus way more than you do.

LAURA *(speaking rudely to* KAT*):* What are you talking about? You've never done anything for anyone else in your entire life. The only person you serve is yourself!

DREW *(to the audience):* When I was born, the doctor told my mom I was the greatest kid to ever grace that hospital. I've always been the greatest!

(*The three of them continue to argue with each other, giving reasons they're each the greatest and the others are not. As they argue, pushing each other around,* JESUS *walks onstage with a bowl of water and a towel. He sets them down as he lines three chairs up CS. He then proceeds to set each person down. He begins with* DREW, *directing him to sit on the chair closest to SL.* DREW *continues talking as he sits, barely acknowledging* JESUS. JESUS *then moves to* LAURA, *leading her to the center seat.*)

LAURA *(speaking to* JESUS *as He directs her):* Oh, hey, Jesus! Yeah, that's right. You tell them I'm the greatest. Tell them all the stuff I do for You. *(She sits down.)*

KAT *(speaking as* JESUS *moves her to the chair closest to SR, motioning for her to sit):* Nobody trusts You like I do, Jesus. You know that.

(JESUS *walks over, picks up the bowl of water and towel, and walks back to* KAT. *He bends down, dips the towel in the water, squeezes it out and washes first one of* KAT's *feet, then the other. As He washes her feet,* KAT *becomes humbled, realizing her selfishness.* JESUS *hands her the bowl and towel and motions for her to wash* LAURA's *feet.* KAT *moves down to* LAURA's *feet as* LAURA *smugly raises her foot to* KAT's *eye level. As* KAT *washes her feet,* LAURA *also becomes humble, realizing she's been wrong. She looks to* JESUS, *who motions to her to take the bowl and towel. She takes them from* KAT, *who moves back to her seat. Then Laura bends down to wash* DREW's *feet. She looks to* JESUS, *who nods, telling her to give the bowl and towel to* DREW. *She then moves back to her seat.* DREW *holds the bowl and towel as* JESUS *speaks.*)

JESUS *(gently but firmly, looking at the other three):* If you love Me, then follow Me.

(JESUS *turns toward SR, looks at the others, waiting for them to follow, then begins to walk offstage as the others slowly get up and follow him off.*)